PURCHASE

poems by

Don Colburn

Finishing Line Press
Georgetown, Kentucky

PURCHASE

A Chapbook of Poems

ACKNOWLEDGMENTS

I thank the publications where these poems first appeared, sometimes in
other versions:

Abandoned Mine: "Self-Portrait?"
American Journal of Poetry: "This Time"
Crosswinds Poetry Journal: "Mentor," "Reach Back" and "Person of Interest"
Galleywinter Poetry Series: "California Gull, State Bird of Utah" and
        "Opposite of Vertigo."
Hubbub: "Voir Dire"
Hunger Mountain: "The Thing About Perfection"
Innisfree: "Distracted by a Man Talking to Himself," "Onlookers at 38th &
        Chicago" and "Keats and I Describe Waterfalls"
Nimrod: "Ginkgo on 19th"
Oberon: "This Very Morning"
Passager: "Pause Over Thanksgiving"
Rat's Ass Review: "Unremarkable" and "A Classroom in Uvalde and a
        Doorstep in K.C."
Southern Poetry Review: "November"
Triggerfish Critical Review: "On the Second Tuesday of December"
Zone 3: "Winter Solstice, Bombay Hook"

Publisher: Leah Huete de Maines
Editor: Christen Kincaid
Cover Photo: Don Colburn, "Sea Smoke off Cape Elizabeth"
Author Photo: Stephanie Yao Long
Cover Design: Elizabeth Maines McCleavy

Order online: www.finishinglinepress.com
        also available on amazon.com

Author inquiries and mail orders:
Finishing Line Press
PO Box 1626
Georgetown, Kentucky 40324
USA

Contents

ONE WORD OR LESS, WHY DO YOU WRITE?

Good question. ERROR! ANSWER EXCEEDS
ALLOWABLE WORD COUNT.
Jeez. Thought you were kidding
about the one word. Give me a minute
to think out loud, don't start counting yet.
How about…Memory? Nope, too vague.
Or…Curiosity? Nah. Too easy and all-purpose.
Mortality? Too grandiose, too woo-woo.
Clarify? Getting warmer. Verbs do that.
But if I were allowed to go way over the limit
and revise, which for me is the best part,
I'd say something about how writing helps you
find answers to questions like this one,
gives you a momentary grip on the world
before it slips free and you start over.
There's a word for this, a noun, maybe a verb—
I just can't come up with it now.
Sometimes it helps to change the subject
so here's one for you: Are you sure it's less
and not fewer? Never mind—stick with less.
Nobody ever says fewer is more.
Less has more juice, more purchasing power
and—wait. Hold on. *Purchase.*

For in the world we jostle—

John Keats, letter to J.H. Reynolds, March 25, 1818

NOVEMBER

Something else to like about this larch
or tamarack if you're from where they call it that
is how last month it blended in
on a hillside unanimous with firs
as if an evergreen. But now
its needles burn alone until they turn
and flourish gold and drop.

Offseason everything's a little off,
ski trails lost without the fact of snow.
The sky today sky-blue, but under foot
dead hoary leaves, hard-rutted mud.
Boulders in the creek necklaced,
skull-capped in ice from overnight.

A season in between, the green of ferns
and leafy hardwoods going if not gone.
And with the sudden waterfall in sight,
it's time to turn around. Footing dicey,
canyon air a spumy not quite rain.
A lot can still go either way.
Sunlight won't matter here for months.

OPPOSITE OF VERTIGO

She says her paintings have three subjects:
body, time, space. In particular
a body's sense of itself in space.
All those big ideas make me wonder
if she's an abstract expressionist,
a phrase I like to say out loud
when all I know is
abstract expressionists hate the label.

Body, time and space more or less
covers it, except there's the mind
or is that understood? I may be overthinking.
On the whitewashed wall
the painter has let shapes of color
express a feeling that has no need
to be understood or named
although she calls this one "Coincidence"

and that one "Tangled Blue."
Is that the scratch it came from
or what became of the day after she sat down
to stare at the light, first thing?
She says it's like the opposite of vertigo,
and looking back at the wall, I get it.
On the news today a baggage handler
thanked God for sitting next to him

as he flew from Charlotte to Dulles
locked in the cargo hold.
How can I not try to imagine
his body's sense of time and space
down in the freezing dark with all that baggage
and into thin air at 35,000 feet?
I bet it felt more like vertigo than the opposite,
though maybe with God in there, both.

CALIFORNIA GULL, STATE BIRD OF UTAH

Oddity abounds in the natural world
before humans get around to renaming it,
so why not give the strange a chance to signify,
as in Utah, where in 1848 skyfuls of seagulls
landed and delivered Mormon pioneers
from a plague of katydids.
The story changes, but the teller always
calls it a miracle, how out of nowhere
or California or islands in Great Salt Lake
they crowded down on half-ruined fields
to gorge themselves, disgorge and gorge again
on black crickets with ornamental wings,
like hosts of heaven and hell contending,
and saved the harvest of peas and beans.

WINTER SOLSTICE, BOMBAY HOOK

What to call this winnowing light
that quickens with the downward sun,

cattails and grasses going copper
to gold? Light we feel before we see

the birds—their grace nonsensical—
frantic-flying cormorants, pintails dabbling

upside-down, the solitary stilted great blue
at the ready, a skidding water-landing loon.

Unworldly calm comes over us inside
the car, no matter what has passed or will

across the boundaries we live within.
We poke along or pull to the shoulder,

engine cut, radio off, windows down,
to better hear the wild wide-angle quiet.

Birdsong in the very names: kingfisher,
bufflehead, merganser, ruddy duck.

Refuge for birds all flyway, flow and habitat;
ours a drive-through afternoon

of make-believe—beatitudes
in riffling marshgrass, mudflats, tidal runs,

two inlet surfaces, roughed-up and glassy
side by side, a crease of wind.

A Dutchman purchased all this
in 1679 for liquor and a gun,

three waistcoats and a kettle.
New Deal duck stamps pieced it back

for waterfowl and us. Bombay Hook
is nothing like the aboriginal Canaresse

for *thicket*, which made more sense.
A gunnery range in World War II made sense

as did the old hotel, hay farms and two lighthouses
until they burned, went bust or washed away.

What's left makes sense at eventide, makes me believe
in sanctuary—and ditches, dikes, impoundments

to hold the water out and in,
a causeway through the light we haven't named.

Across the bay, a pale moon rises poised
above the cooling tower's hourglass,

while opposite, the timely sun breaks through again
and a spackling of cloud that held back afternoon

becomes a smudge, promising
to pass through every shade before full dark,

late in the day arriving earlier
and earlier until tomorrow.

PERSON OF INTEREST

Before we knew to be afraid,
back in the postwar I Like Ike '50s,
guns were riflery at summer camp in Maine.
Prone on the floor of the firing range
over near the dump, we aimed our .22's
at perfect circles 50 feet away.
The prize for bull's eyes? Bragging rights,
Marksman medals, sew-on merit badges.
My best friend at camp was Billy Johnson
from Lewiston. Billy was unbeatable
at cockfighting, hopping around the campfire
till he was the last boy standing on one leg.
Where is he now, with Lewiston
and much of Maine on lockdown, a killer
on the loose? Not Billy, of course,
though when I heard "Lewiston,"
memory for an instant downloaded Billy
circa 1959, blowing a pink balloon
of bubble gum big as his head
as if to buffer the breaking
news: 18 shot dead in a bowling alley
and a billiards bar. Should I lock down?
I'm 30 miles from where the Person of Interest
ditched his Outback at a boat launch
on the Androscoggin. I'm allergic to euphemisms,
but tonight I respect their soft pedal.
Shooting spree, suspect at large, shelter in place.
Dark Day for Maine, the headline says.
Manhunt. All points bulletin. Infra red.
Person of Interest, if he's alive,
is the only one who knows where.
Flyovers, divers, dogs. No wind, no rain,
the weather itself a euphemism,
perfect late fall days called Indian summer
whether or not we've had the killing frost.

DISTRACTED BY A MAN TALKING TO HIMSELF

We're on a bus stuck in traffic,
wrong side of the river.
At least I have something to read.
He's directly across, speaking nonstop.
I want to get back to my book
of poems by one of the greats
I've tried hard to understand
but that won't work now
with this other voice in the way
whose words I don't quite catch
yet can't stop listening for,
the tone so true that if I heard it
through a flimsy motel wall I'd know
his need. Know if he was pissed
or plastered or deliriously glad,
singing to himself or chatting up
a woman. Know if she was there
or on the phone or in the bathtub
with the door ajar—or on a bus
inside his talking head and mine.

SELF-PORTRAIT?

The emcee for tonight's reading beckons me
out of the coffee line, brandishing her notepad.
Wants me to know that introducing poets
is a waste of time for everyone.
How could I not like Terri, her lack of slack,
her tone so right-on that I take her seriously
even if she's joking. Today her hair is purple.
Would she say lilac? Maybe lavender.
Here's my idea, she says, and I'm all ears:
No book titles, no prizes nobody's heard of.
No "debut" or "garnered" or "iconic." No blurbs.
I'll ask each of you one simple question
and your quick-and-easy will be the whole shebang.
So…If you were a punctuation mark…

and I flinch. I see Barbara Walters on TV
ask Hepburn what kind of tree she was.
Trick question, I say to myself, overthinking.
Probably not a semi-colon is what comes out
first. I'm stalling, still in need of coffee.
Terri nods expectantly. Not an exclamation point
is my next attempt to keep truth in play
without letting it box me in. Her nod this time
gives a hint of miff. Not a comma either, I plod on,
and now Terri's annoyed, her brilliant ploy
foundering on a poet's refusal to follow directions.
Time's up, she snaps. Her felt-tip pen lands
on the pad with a flourishing curl and a jab
to put me down as question mark.

VOIR DIRE

No one knows except the man
who sits there in cuffed silence
and may not be innocent
though in our minds he must be
until proven otherwise
and no one else is allowed
to weigh in on what happened
except the lawyer wagging
his doubt-free index finger
and making eye contact with
every last one of us
or the assistant D.A.
who just said the opposite
so one of them is lying
and it will be up to us.

If they ask me under oath
whether I can see both sides
will I have the guts to say
that once we bring it all down
to two words or just the one
and the man is led away
uncuffed or cuffed, and after
the judge thanks us one last time
I can go back to where days
are for the most part moot and
not numbered, not exactly,
and pour a tall glass, step out
onto the back patio
in clarifying twilight
and wonder is it ever
beyond reasonable doubt?

MENTOR

for Simone Di Piero

Isn't this what we all wish for?
you said as you swiped a rag across
the chalky blackboard, erasing
old scores. We were throwing darts
against the back wall of a dive
on the edge of downtown,
you and me and JD, all in our 30s,
which made us dangerously old.
It was loud and dark and—this was years ago—
smoky throughout.
Feathery darts hit bull's-eyes or missed,
some not even close. No one got hurt.

How we loved those meaningless tallies.
My pint lasted a triple header
until we took a table closer to the bar
and switched from darts to liar's dice.
We rattled and spilled our dice cups,
then bluffed, held, caved
and called each other out. More scores,
more clean slates that didn't count.
One that did would be there in the morning
as you sat on a stiff-backed chair,
pencil in hand—this was years ago—
to stare down another blank page.

HOMEWARD ON THE CROSS SOUND FERRY

The *Cape Henlopen* backs out so fluently
I don't notice until the muggy air stirs.
Weekenders loll on deck chairs
oblivious to ghosts in the ramps
and gangways down on the car deck.
A black dot sliding sideways
off to starboard becomes a cormorant
as I make my way to the cafe lounge.

So many things in this temporal world
have nothing to do with each other
until their timely crisscross in our ken—
like the greatest amphibious invasion in history
and a solitary cormorant seen over the railing
of a ferry built 80 years ago for war.

If you don't remember, the lounge walls do:
a grainy panorama of maps, cutaways,
blown-up photos and front page news
gray as the foggy D-Day dawn off Normandy
where floating boxcars disgorge armed men
to their waists in the cold choppy sea.
Their first goal: make it to the beach.
Then join others, fuzzy in the distance,
ants in their slow scurry, hell-bent,
anything to stay upright in motion.

That evening the President prayed aloud
over the radio in my parents' living room.
Let our hearts be stout
to wait out the long travail.
I wasn't there
till now, staring at banner headlines
ALLIED ARMIES LAND IN FRANCE;
GREAT INVASION IS UNDER WAY

and foggy images of this vessel
under a different name in a past life,
unloading war.

What did they know, the young
helmeted men in the bloody waters
or on Omaha beach? They knew
the each-and-all of infantry, and knew
not everyone would get back home.

ONLOOKERS AT 38TH & CHICAGO

Before George Floyd, I always found a way
with someone on the news about to die
to close my eyes or turn and look away.

But now I've watched that video ricochet
and cannot turn my head hard as I try
each time before George Floyd passes away.

He doesn't pass away. They kill him splayed
face down beside the right rear tire, his eyes
ablaze with terror, calling *Mama*, airway

choked off, cop kneeling on his neck, no way
to turn his head. Three men in blue stand by.
Before George Floyd they always found some way

to say the dead man was a threat to put away
for good. *Can't breathe…*, his hoarse whisper a cry
to officers who look, and look away.

Onlookers all, we can't unhear his *Why?*
Bystanders? No excuse for standing by.
George Floyd, dying, showed us another way.
He couldn't close his eyes or look away.

THIS TIME

after Christchurch

Far side of the world this time, he knows just when the most
worshipers will be at the mosques.

This time 50, while they prayed. The 50th not found in the pileup
of bodies until the next day.

The youngest this time a 3-year-old Somali boy wearing white
socks with no-slip grips on the bottom as he runs toward
gunfire thinking it's a video game.

The dead from 11 countries.

He live-streams it from a camera mounted on his head, leaving
his hands free to fire more rounds.

This time he survives.

I swear I won't fall into the madman's trap, won't give him that
satisfaction. This time I can't help myself.

He's 28. The mug shot has downcast eyes and short, light-brown
hair. He's a member of Anytime Fitness 24-hour gym.

He had "a regular childhood." Grew up uncomfortable around
girls, his best friends computers. His father is a garbage
collector who competes in ironman triathlons. There is no
mention of his mother.

This time he lives in a modest pale blue-gray house outside
Dunedin. It has air conditioning units and wide windows with
curtains left open. The yard is overgrown and the mailbox has
a sticker "NO JUNK MAIL Thank you!"

His ex-lawyer says he seems lucid and unimpaired "other than
holding fairly extreme views."

He doesn't display any regret.

The vice president of the Rifle Club where he practiced says he's polite and helps put things away.

His family's first inkling comes when they see him on the TV news. His grandmother says they are all gobsmacked.

He has five firearms he obtained legally, including two semi-automatic assault rifles. The prime minister vows to change the gun laws this time. Gun purchases surge.

Facebook teams work through the night to remove more than a million copies of the video multiplying after the massacre. This time they can't keep up.

He posts a 74-page manifesto full of sarcasm, memes, hate sites and trolls. He urges followers to "paint, write, sing, dance, recite poetry." It's hard to tell when he's joking, and he mixes up "effect" and "affect."

This time he vows to see us next in Valhalla.

A CLASSROOM IN UVALDE AND A DOORSTEP IN KC

A 10-year-old named Noah somehow kept his head
when Room 112 became a screaming bloody hell.
Noah knew that to survive he must play dead.

The shooter fired away, kids fell and falling bled.
Were any still alive? Eyes shut, Noah couldn't tell.
The 10-year-old lay still and somehow kept his head.

A teen named Ralph couldn't know what lay ahead
when in the dark he rang the wrong door bell.
Ralph didn't know that to survive he must play dead.

Mr. Lester, 84 and scared, got up from bed,
peered out and saw a young black face, the telltale "tell."
He fired twice without troubling to keep his head.

"People come to my door all the time," his neighbor said.
All sorts, from all around, some with stuff to sell,
even a stranger lost—"I don't shoot them in the head."

More lockdowns with our flags half-mast, more blood shed
in schools, on doorsteps—grief a habit learned too well.
A 10-year-old named Noah somehow kept his head.
Survival, we all now know, requires playing dead.

BEST MAN

In our booth in the bar Jimmie looks bigger,
arms buff and brawny, eyes ice blue.
Meeting here was my idea, a safe place
to talk, nothing but Budweisers
between us on the dark shellac.
Jimmie did time in the Florida state pen
and all I've heard is one word: murder.
Now my friend is set to marry him
and I have questions, though I said yes
right away—tell me you wouldn't—
when they asked me to be best man.

I did it for the money, Jimmie says.
Murder for hire. Dumbly I nod
and swig, give his answer its chance
to lower the stakes for the best man.
His voice flat, unshellacked.
It happened years ago, a line
we've all used to turn down heat.
I'm glad to hear there was another murder
Jimmie said no to. Too risky, he says,
which in our booth sounds reasonable,
a wise move, maybe even brave.
Jimmie talks through another round
without taking the Fifth. I'm a groomsman,
not a judge, my only plea bargain
with myself. Outside on the sidewalk
we shake on the deal we've made.

'BE WHERE YOUR FEET ARE'

from 'Best Advice' of New York Times readers

There are 26 bones in the human foot
which is absurd—the 26 bones.
No wonder it hurts so easily. Out for a walk,
I come to one of those eye-level boxes on a pole
in front of a neighbor's gone-by rose bush.
A sucker for signs, I lean in
to find under plexiglass a short poem

about writing a 10-volume history of weather.
Which is absurd—the 10 volumes—
but William James Collins, who goes by Billy,
knew I'd believe every word. Here I am
at a stand-still, squinting, grounded,
all 52 weight-bearing bones down there
doing the job without attention to themselves.

KEATS AND I DESCRIBE WATERFALLS

Dark water from somewhere above
is how it starts and will not stop,
over whaleback granite ledges, down
to where it runs out of rock
and plunges silverly into the lake—
silverly a word I wouldn't think of
if John Keats hadn't first
in a letter to his younger brother, Tom.
Everything in motion, even the lake,
greenish with rock flour, wind-roughed
and drifting toward a logjam.

In the summer of 1818, Keats walked north
across Scotland and saw waterfalls
for the first time. His fervent fancy
held still for once, no match for the real.
The sight of so much falling water
astonished him, he told Tom,
its tone and color *or if I may so say,*
the intellect. It would not stop.
Back home in Hampstead, Tom was dying
of consumption, and Keats apologized

for describing what he'd seen.
Descriptions are bad, he wrote,
but *I shall learn poetry here.*
None of this made sense
until this afternoon as I sat on a log
by a crook in the Nooksack's north fork
to watch a never-ending cataract
of greenish whitewater spill silverly
over boulders in a riverbed
and fancied something restless,
beyond description, out of sight.

ON THE SECOND TUESDAY OF DECEMBER

Steve, we went ahead anyway
with this month's Old Farts lunch
on Zoom. Greg told about fly-fishing
with you in the Wallowas and over in Idaho,
and doubling down on a riffle in the Imnaha
or Grande Ronde. How you fished in style,
chest-high waders and in your knapsack
a Mason jar of martinis for later
with cigars around the campfire.

So different from how we knew you at the paper,
always on deadline, all business, chasing new leads,
another day trying to explain the world
to the world. Or was it? Didn't we all fish
those troubled waters for stories?
You did a good job of it, this living,
including the kicker at the end.
Remember the last time we talked?
Once we got done with the crappy weather
and the election, I finally dared ask.
"Getting by," you said, so plainly
I didn't know you were saying goodbye.

          Even now, forgive me,
when I think of the parting glass you raised
days later to your lips while you still could,
I picture you at a bend in the river
up to your waist in swift water
as you cast your last looping line out
and wait for it to thrill with attention
from something below the surface,
a cutthroat or maybe a rainbow.

REACH BACK

for R.A.N., turning 80

Now late in summer, one of your four
favorite seasons, reach back with me
for music from the past, that muscle memory—
cello, bassoon, recorder, voice,
their notes and what comes in between.
And now that recent nows can seem a ways
away, reach back beyond. Down East
one foggy morning, the fingers of your hand
described an evergreen in wind so well
I saw the wind. You taught me how to tell
a nun from a can—which I still know—
and ketch from yawl, which I no longer know
and helped me build a tiny boat
of balsa wood, a staple for its tiller, thread for lines.
Grace at dinner was time to ask for strength
and courage for whatever was to come
and know we'd need them both. Reach back.
When you leaped and danced in drizzle
to see a treetop eagle on the Skagit flats,
the eagle was impressed. What verve!
It runs through everything you do.
Split wood. Set sail. Swim in the cold sea.
You joined the big words seamlessly:
teach and learn, music and medicine, life
and livelihood. Physician? Teacher? One.
On your kitchen table one Saturday
an oval Plaster of Paris blob
hardened inside a blue balloon—
your model of the human brain.
Reach back and let the stories tell.
Swallows and Amazons, Bert and I, Flanders
and Swann, E. B. White and L.L. Bean.
A letter from the Jersey poet, Dr. Williams.
Blue Hill, Back Bay, Big Dig, World's End.
Remember? Off Marblehead, with Jo,
you taught me to head up into the wind.

THIS VERY MORNING

'Very' is the most useless word...and can always come out.
—Florence King

Philip got right back to thank me
for sending his way a good wish
and timely because he was rushing out
to say goodbye to an old friend.
He had to get to the ICU
and be done before 10 a.m.
when the other part was set to happen.
Philip, who lives in a flood zone
near a landfall for hurricanes
and has written books on hundred-year storms,
race riots and several wars,
said it somehow seems wrong
they can schedule things like that,

meaning the very end of a life.
It's almost 10 their time, or his.
What good is my good wish now
as he leans over a bed in a curtained-off bay,
trying to bid farewell
to someone with a tube down his throat
who probably can't hear
the whoosh and wheeze of makeshift breath.
Bet this happens more than you think
is a thought I won't share with Philip
when I write back this very afternoon,
starting with useless words.

ALMOST THERE IN DEEP PARTIAL

By a fire pit on the edge of totality
I wait with friends for the world
to look new. Darkness a rumor.
We fuss with flimsy safety glasses,
except Bill, who leans back in his lawn chair
and steadies a Navy sextant on his nose.
Liz tilts a colander on the stone wall
just so, to spray pinhole polka dots
onto a poster, tiny suns etched
by moon shadow into upside down hearts.
Wouldn't it be crazy, Dick muses,
to have an earthquake right now.

Whatever's going on up there remains
a mystery—something about the moon
getting in the way of daylight
like clouds do all the time.
Whirligigs in orbit—moon around earth
around sun—late or soon align.
And look! The sun's a snickerdoodle
with a bite missing. Down here
it's not quite darkness I feel
but a brittle stillness in the light.
We should have gone upstate to Caribou
or Millinocket, deeper in the swath.

This 96.4 percent totality sounds dark
but underestimates the sun. Upon review
"deep partial" gets to nowhere near complete.
In high school English, Mr. Eaton ("Moth")
knew the meaning of not quite. We showed him
every day. He never gave a grade above 90—
to leave us room. Almost there
is where I've spent most of my life.
At 3:33 p.m., still no corona, no apocalypse.
Slight chill, a hint of dusk, with room enough
for sun to slip the obfuscating moon
and give us back a Monday afternoon.

THE THING ABOUT PERFECTION

in memory of Don Larsen

The thing about perfection
is how nobody sees it coming
except those destined for disappointment.
A journeyman hurler, brush cut and big ears,
whose teammates call him Gooney Bird,
goes out-and-out untouchable one fall afternoon
and 63 years later his obit in the *Times*
has to say perfect a dozen ways.

He wasn't scheduled to pitch
Game 5, Dodgers and Yankees,
until he opened his locker and found
a warm-up ball in one of his cleats,
the manager's unspoken code.

The best he could hope for
was to keep the Yanks in the game
against Jackie and Campy, Pee Wee
and Duke. But by the top of the fifth,
goose eggs accumulating, the crowd
began to murmur and buzz.
In the dugout they shunned him,
no chatter, no eye contact, nothing
to jinx what might be happening.
Skill played a role, of course,
and skill's uppity cousin, luck.
Mantle robbed Hodges deep in left center.
A hot grounder caromed perfectly
off the third baseman to the shortstop
and Robinson was out by half a step.
Amoros's homer hooked a few inches foul.
The final pitch wasn't a strike, but he got the call.
Yogi ran out in full catcher's gear and leaped
into his arms, nearly obliterating him
in the perfect front-page photo.

Then came the hard part, the rest of his life,
perfect strangers mistaking one game
for the whole ordinary story, 15 seasons,
seven teams, more losses than wins.
Soon he was in extra innings, a second career
out in California selling cardboard boxes.
He learned what to say when anyone wondered.
"Goofy things happen," he said.
"Everyone's entitled to some good days."

UNREMARKABLE

Like when the sun comes up again,
vague in fog, a fuzzy far-off ball
slowly burning up, mid-size
among the Milky Way's 100 billion stars.

Except it's ours and who am I
to call it unremarkable—big belittling word
with a backwards knack for reminding you
what isn't there or might have been

remarked on. My father's testicles
were unremarkable, on the last page
of the autopsy. (Dear Coroner:
You don't owe your life to them.)

The Las Vegas gambler on the 32nd floor
who opened fire on country music fans
was unremarkable, the sheriff said.
In the history of days, today

is unremarkable, yet somewhere
lightning goes to ground. A wayward look
across the table changes everything.
In a room without windows the jury deadlocks.

Luck after all these years is time
to sip another mug of coffee, room for cream,
and call a new day unremarkable,
in praise.

PAUSE OVER THANKSGIVING

November 2023

Out of rubble, dust and untold awful
numbers comes a four-day-maybe pause.
Not a ceasefire. Do not call it that.
One Israeli hostage freed for every three
Palestinian prisoners let go by Israel.

First, numbers without names. Then lists.
Then names with faces on Day One.
Thirteen Israelis, women and children first.
Thirty-nine Palestinians in exchange.
Not a ceasefire. Do not call it that.

Some names will come alive: Yafa. Margalit,
Hana, Adina. Daniel, Emilia, Doron. Raz, Aviv,
Channa. Ruth. Karen. Ohad. Not Avigail,
who's 4 and watched her parents murdered.
Her name is somewhere on a list.

So many others lost or unaccounted for
between the river and the sea. The killing
intimate, bombs and rockets indiscriminate.
Twelve hundred on Oct. 7, twelve thousand since,
a million or more displaced from home.

Here at our bountiful table, safe, we pause,
say grace and pray for peace across the world
where, once the other pause begins, a mother says,
"We're happy, but we dare not celebrate."
You cannot tell which side she's on.

GINKGO ON 19th

in memory of William Trevor

End of November, end of what Auden
would call a low dishonest year,
my legs and meds working well enough
to roam the neighborhood
while cold rain holds off.
Most of the leaves down, stuck
to the sidewalk with old rain;
they'll never dry out, never skitter.
The piles in the street are soggy bran.
But right there on the other side of 19th,
a little ginkgo stands out, brilliant yellow,
its leaves holding on, or is it the tree
holding on? Another imponderable
in this ordinary afternoon, this dark time.
I think of the ordinary stories you told,
how lovely and sad they became
without need of symbols,
how you believed in not quite knowing,
and how there is always, always
as you said in a made-up true story
a little more to it than that.

NOTES

I'm grateful to the artists retreat at Yaddo, where some of these poems came into being. Hearty thanks also to John Morrison and Dave Jarecki for their encouragement and smarts in the spirit and living memory of Peter Sears. Above all, love and gratitude to Nell—best reader and trail magic personified.

"The Thing About Perfection" won the Ruth Stone Poetry Prize, awarded by *Hunger Mountain.*

"November" also appeared in the *Portland Press Herald*'s Deep Water poetry column.

The italicized line in "California Gull, State Bird of Utah" is from Orson Whitney's *History of Utah.*

"This Time" refers to mass shootings at two mosques in New Zealand on March 15, 2019. The gunman killed 51 people and injured 40 more.

"Voir Dire," from the French for "speak truth," refers to interrogation of potential jurors before a trial. For this particular trial, I was questioned but not selected as a juror.

Florence King (epigraph in "This Very Morning") was a writer, described in her 2016 *New York Times* obituary as a "columnist, author and professional misanthrope."

Don Colburn came to poetry late, in the midst of a newspaper career. A longtime reporter for *The Washington Post* and *The Oregonian*, he was a finalist for the Pulitzer Prize in feature writing. He has come to view journalism and poetry, for all their differences, as complementary ways of witness and truth-telling. He's a graduate of Amherst College and has an MFA degree in poetry from the Program for Writers at Warren Wilson College. *Purchase* is Colburn's sixth poetry collection; all six won or placed in national manuscript contests. His full-length book, *As If Gravity Were a Theory*, won the Cider Press Review Book Award, and his first chapbook, *Another Way to Begin*, won the Finishing Line Press Poetry Prize. *Mortality, With Pronoun Shifts* received the Cathy Smith Bowers chapbook award. Another collection, *Tomorrow Too: The Brenda Monologues*, is a sequence of informal sonnets based on the true story of a young woman facing breast cancer while pregnant—a story he first reported in *The Oregonian*. Other honors include the Discovery/*The Nation* Award, a Knight Journalism Fellowship at Stanford University, the Blethen Award for Distinguished Newspaper Reporting, the Ruth Stone Poetry Prize and residencies at MacDowell and Yaddo. He lives with his wife, Nell, in Falmouth, Maine.

For more info or to contact Don Colburn: *www.doncolburn.net*.

www.ingramcontent.com/pod-product-compliance
Lightning Source LLC
Chambersburg PA
CBHW022045080426
42734CB00009B/1243